Waikīkī

IMAGES OF YESTERYEAR

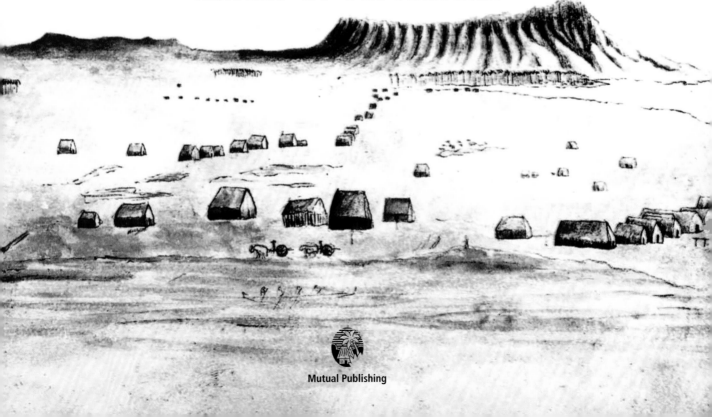

Mutual Publishing

The smallpox epidemic in Hawai'i began in May 1853 and ended in January 1854, claiming 6,000 lives, tragically reducing the very venerable native population. This tiny grass shack in Waikīkī, whose exact location is unknown, served as the only hospital. Waikīkī was then considered a place of healing, with regenerative powers.

DRAWING BY PAUL EMMERT. HAWAIIAN HISTORICAL SOCIETY

PREVIOUS PAGE: *A view of Diamond Head from across the flatlands of Mō'ili'ili. Circa 1840.* TONGG PUBLISHING

ISBN-10: 1-56647-824-3
ISBN-13: 978-1-56647-824-3
Library of Congress Catalog Card Number: 2007902793

First Printing, July 2007
1 2 3 4 5 6 7 8 9

Mutual Publishing, LLC
1215 Center Street, Suite 210
Honolulu, Hawai'i 96816
Ph: 808-732-1709 / Fax: 808-734-4094
Email: info@mutualpublishing.com
www.mutualpublishing.com

Printed in China

This 1850s lithograph by G.H. Burgess shows community life in Waikīkī. The men in the foreground prepare fishing canoes and nets as others return from the ocean. Women collect limu (seaweed) and tend to keiki (children). The Hawaiian culture was one of communal sharing, with each member of the extended village family contributing to the prosperity of the whole.
BISHOP MUSEUM

Pāʻū riders were a common sight in 1850s Waikīkī. HAWAIʻI STATE ARCHIVES

An interpretation of surfing by someone unfamiliar with the sport that nevertheless captures the excitement of riding waves. Surfers glide along the face of a rising wave, not straight down along its breaking curl. At the time, boards of 5 to 15 feet long were crafted into elongated "tombstone" shapes and stained with the pounded bark of kukui nut trees. Circa 1872.
BISHOP MUSEUM

King Kamehameha V's grass-thatched cottage was located among the famous 10,000-tree coconut grove at Helumoa, which laced through Waikīkī's entire royal acreage. After his death in 1872, his beachfront kauhale (housing compound) continued to serve as a royal retreat. The Seaside Hotel and later the Royal Hawaiian Hotel were built on these grounds, and remnants of the grove still stand in the east courtyard of the Royal Hawaiian Hotel. In the foreground is the ʻĀpuakēhau Stream, fed by waters that drained from the mountain valleys of Mānoa, Makiki, and Pālolo. Circa 1870. HAWAIʻI STATE ARCHIVES

6

The Waikīkī home of Princess Bernice Pauahi Bishop was on the Kamehameha lands at Helumoa. Circa 1880. HAWAI'I STATE ARCHIVES

Daughter of a mixed-race marriage, educated in England, and an accomplished musician, artist, and linguist, the young and graceful Princess Kaʻiulani embodied the spirit of her times. Here she poses at her ʻĀinahau estate (near the site of the present-day Princess Kaʻiulani Hotel) with Prince David Kawananakoa (her cousin), Eva Parker (a friend), and Rose Cleghorn (her half-sister). HAWAIʻI STATE ARCHIVES

Princess Kaʻiulani was born in 1875 as the Kingdom of Hawaiʻi began its end. She was beautiful both as a child and later as a young woman. The daughter of Princess Miriam Likelike and Archibald S. Cleghorn, and the niece of King Kalākaua and Queen Liliʻuokalani, her life in many ways symbolized the Hawaiian nation for which she was groomed to serve as heir apparent; unfortunately, she died at age twenty-four. HAWAIʻI STATE ARCHIVES

One of the most famous lūʻau in Hawaiian history was hosted by King Kalākaua, in honor of Robert Louis Stevenson and his mother. Seated next to the King is his sister, the future Queen Liliʻuokalani. The February 1889 event took place at "Manuia Lānai," the Henry Poor residence in Waikīkī. BAKER-VAN DYKE COLLECTION

From the peak of Diamond Head, Waikīkī is dominated by the immense racetrack that served as a playground for Honolulu's wealthy residents and later became Kapiʻolani Park. In the distance is the shadowed mound of Punchbowl crater, and the sparsely populated coastline of Honolulu. Circa 1890. BISHOP MUSEUM

The serenity of old Waikīkī is captured in this photo. Circa 1900s. BAKER-VAN DYKE COLLECTION

Waikīkī fishermen wait for the next wave to help push their canoe to higher ground. The pier in the background, built by developer W.C. Peacock, had just been completed when this photo was taken in 1890. HAWAI'I STATE ARCHIVES

Near the turn of the nineteenth century, cottage-style retreats, like the Occidental Hotel at Waikīkī, came into existence. Here wealthy families and members of the Hawaiian aliʻi took shelter during their long, relaxing days on the beach. These Victorian summer cottages were "sparsely" furnished according to the brocade-tapestry style of the day. They were all eventually supplanted by bigger hotels. BISHOP MUSEUM

Waikīkī keiki (children) take a break in their play to pose at the mouth of the Kuʻekaunahi Stream. This waterway flowed along what is now Kapahulu Avenue and emptied at Kūhiō Beach where the jettied drainage pipe now stands. Circa 1886.

A. MITCHELL, BISHOP MUSEUM

The Park-Beach Hotel, previously the Macfarlane residence, located near the beach fronting Diamond Head. Circa 1890.
RAY JEROME BAKER COLLECTION, BISHOP MUSEUM

Surfers still strike a pose much like this today waiting for the next set, looking out for the next perfect wave—its size and swell direction. Notice the seaweed (now uncommon) lining the beach and the size and shape of the surfboard. Circa 1889.
FRANK DAVEY, BISHOP MUSEUM

The end of the mule-drawn tramcar line, located at the expansive bridge where the present-day Kapahulu Avenue meets Kalākaua Avenue. The sign above reads, "Driving faster than a walk over the bridge will be prosecuted according to the law." The 1905 Territorial Legislature changed the name of Waikīkī Road, the main artery linking Waikīkī with downtown Honolulu, to Kalākaua Avenue. Circa 1890s. BAKER COLLECTION, BISHOP MUSEUM

An electric trolley breezes along over the wide-open landscape toward Waikīkī. These speedy trolleys cut travel time from downtown by at least a third. The Honolulu Rapid Transit Company trolleys serviced Waikīkī from 1903 until 1941 when they were replaced by buses. Circa 1901. EMMA I. RICKEY, BAKER-VAN DYKE COLLECTION

Duck ponds along with rice paddies dominated the foreground of Waikīkī. Circa 1913. BISHOP MUSEUM

The water sports of ancient Hawai‘i fascinated visitors to the world-famous beach. Early images used to attract tourists were panoramas like this one of canoes and surfboards. Circa 1910–1915. HAWAIIAN HISTORICAL SOCIETY

When this photo was taken, Waikīkī had established itself as a world-class tourist destination. The Moana Hotel (far left), then the island's only big hostelry outside of downtown Honolulu, boasted a fine-dining room on the beach and a famous pier. To its right are the Hustace Villa, the Cleghorn and Steiner properties, and the Waikīkī Tavern. Circa 1910. ALONZO GARTLEY, BISHOP MUSEUM

With its wrap-around verandah and high-roofed Victorian turret, "the Longworth cottage" was the largest at the Seaside Hotel, so named because Nicholas Longworth and his wife, Alice Roosevelt, daughter of President Teddy Roosevelt, stayed here. This Ray Jerome Baker photo became a famous postcard. Circa 1908. BAKER-VAN DYKE COLLECTION

By the early 1900s, the sugar barons along with members of the wealthy elite began to build "beach homes" unparalleled in size, opulence, and grandeur in Waikīkī. One of the most beautiful was Kainalu, the mansion of James B. Castle built in 1899 on the beach near Diamond Head. Designed by Oliver P. Traphagen, it included a breakfast room made of dark koa wood, a rooftop garden, and a lānai supported by beams that jutted over the water. Circa 1905. CHRISTIAN HEDEMANN, BISHOP MUSEUM

Private homes to the right of the Moana Hotel, 1913. BISHOP MUSEUM

"With smoking crests," a "bull-mouthed monster" steams toward present-day Queen's beach, to metaphor writer Jack London's impressions of Waikīkī waves. Circa 1915. RAY JEROME BAKER COLLECTION, BISHOP MUSEUM

Paddle crews and their spectators throng the beach at the finish line of an outrigger canoe race. Such regattas became a mainstay of Waikīkī Beach activities, attracting canoe clubs from all over the Islands. Circa 1914. BISHOP MUSEUM

The Hau Tree Lanai at the Halekulani Hotel. The hau, a lowland tree of the hibiscus variety, could be trained on trellises to form a tangled, curling-branched roof. 1919. BAKER-VAN DYKE COLLECTION

The McInerney beach cottage acquired by the McInerneys in 1903. Circa 1910. C.J. HEDERMANN COLLECTION, BISHOP MUSEUM

The western-most end of Waikīkī Beach, the future site of the Hilton Hawaiian Village. Originally the John Ena home on Kālia Road, the property underwent several transitions. The later cottages and a relandscaped six acres became the Niumalu (Sheltering Palms) Hotel, which accommodated up to 125 guests and included a dining room and dance floor in the central complex. In turn, the Niumalu Hotel was replaced by the world-class Hilton Hawaiian Village. 1920. BAKER-VAN DYKE COLLECTION

"The First Lady of Waikīkī," the Moana Hotel was Waikīkī's first successful luxurious overnight accommodation. The original hotel, a five-story wooden building fronting Kalākaua Avenue, opened in 1901. By 1918, it was expanded with the addition of two wings costing $530,000, which more than doubled the hotel's capacity to accommodate the growing number of tourists seeking the "magic of Waikīkī." While the Moana was "the" center of Waikīkī, most of the surrounding areas were still swamps or taro fields, as the Ala Wai Canal had not yet been built. HAWAI'I STATE ARCHIVES

The Royal Hawaiian opened on February 1, 1927, with a series of parties, the likes of which Hawaiʻi had never seen before, or since. The "Pink Palace" towered over its neighbors, and with the Moana, dominated Waikīkī's palm-filled skyline. Its four hundred rooms, each with a bath, balcony, and mountain or ocean views, almost doubled the guest occupancy of Waikīkī. Very much a product of Roaring Twenties sensibilities, the "Pink Palace" offered a more avant-garde approach to the hostelry business. While its neighbor, the Moana, clung to an image of Victorian conservatism, the Royal presaged the glitzy flash and accelerated hoopla that became Waikīkī's trademark. BAKER-VAN DYKE COLLECTION

A 1933 aerial view of Diamond Head and Waikīkī showing the Royal Hawaiian and Moana Hotels. BISHOP MUSEUM

In this 1930 image, a trolley moves along Kalākaua Avenue just in front of the Cleghorn beach house. Already the bungalow-style houses that would so characterize Waikīkī's neighborhoods had begun to proliferate on the mauka (mountain) side of the street. These quaint cottages would eventually disappear, casualties of the high-rise construction frenzy that would sweep through Waikīkī in the sixties and seventies. KODAK HAWAII, BISHOP MUSEUM

A group of accommodating surfers pose for a visitor's Kodak camera box. JEROME BAKER COLLECTION, BISHOP MUSEUM

Duke Kahanamoku (far right) and his brothers (left to right: Bill, Sam, Louis, David, and Sergeant) pose in front of the old Moana Bathhouse, Waikīkī, in 1928. A strong traditionalist, Duke also favored the 16-foot, solid koa wood surfboards of ancient design. TAI SING LOO, BISHOP MUSEUM

In this late-1930s view taken from the Royal Hawaiian, the change in bathing suits from earlier times can be seen.
FARBMAN, BISHOP MUSEUM

Tree-lined streets with small cottages were typical in Waikīkī before the tourist boom of the '60s replaced them. In 1940, Kaʻiulani Avenue was a quiet street. RAY JEROME BAKER COLLECTION, BISHOP MUSEUM

During the war, the Moana and Royal Hawaiian Hotels became "rest and recreation" lodging for servicemen, many of whom dried their underwear and socks in the windows. Barbed wire was placed along Waikīkī Beach soon after the Pearl Harbor attack to guard against possible Japanese seaborne invasion. Martial law went into effect on December 8, 1941, and lasted until October 24, 1944, when the threat of invasion had long since diminished. The barbed wire barriers came down in 1943.

BAKER-VAN DYKE COLLECTION

The cluster of coconut trees on the beach fronting Kalākaua Avenue near Uluniu Street was eventually thinned to make space for new hostelries, taverns, and imported banyans. Trolley tracks, sunken into the paved asphalt, made the street bumpy for the new Fords and Chevys. Circa 1945. RAY JEROME BAKER COLLECTION, BISHOP MUSEUM

Two-way Kalākaua Avenue still allowed parking in the 1960s. LAURENCE HATA COLLECTION, BISHOP MUSEUM

Throughout the years Waikīkī also became known for the colorful people who visited, frequented, lived, or worked there. The cast of characters included celebrities, locals, everyday people, surfers, beachboys, and bathing beauties. Well-dressed visitors would grace Waikīkī's boulevards, hotels, and restaurants wearing coats and ties. Today, the only suits found in Waikīkī are the scanty bathing ones. Outside restaurant and hotel lobby signs read, "Footwear and shirts must be worn." From left to right: L.P. Thurston, George "Dad" Center, unidentified, Douglas Fairbanks, Mary Pickford, and Duke Kahanamoku, 1929. TAI SING LOO, BISHOP MUSEUM

(1) Dressed in a maritime vest, a European-style hat and a traditional malo (loincloth), this Hawaiian carries his calabash. Circa 1852. BAKER-VAN DYKE COLLECTION (2) By the end of the nineteenth century, surfing was at its lowest ebb, having been banned by the missionary influence. This lone surfer carries one of the last alaia boards. DAVEY, BISHOP MUSEUM (3) Being playful in a Hawaiian thatched hut at Helumoa. BAKER-VAN DYKE COLLECTION

(1) *The rich and the famous came to Waikīkī in the 1920s to enjoy what was becoming the world's best-known beach. His Royal Highness Albert Edward, Prince of Wales, the future King Edward VIII, donning a Moana Hotel bathing suit, could not resist a ride in a Hawaiian outrigger canoe.* BISHOP MUSEUM (2) *Jack London and his wife, Charmian (sitting next to him), relax on the beach at the Outrigger Canoe Club with their friends and host Alexander Hume Ford in 1915. London tried for several hours to catch a wave, succeeding only in giving himself a severe sunburn.* BAKER-VAN DYKE COLLECTION (3) *This 1915 photo of Duke Kahanamoku at the Outrigger Canoe Club influenced sculptor Jan Fisher for his statue of Duke that now stands at Kūhiō Beach.* BAKER-VAN DYKE COLLECTION

(1) Bing Crosby rides a scooter in front of the Royal Hawaiian Hotel during a break in shooting the film Waikiki Wedding. *1935.* TAI SING LOO, BISHOP MUSEUM *(2) When the U.S. entered the war in 1941, the government forbade most photography. Many of the over 250,000 members of the armed forces stationed at one point or another in Hawai'i poured into the studios of photographer Ray Jerome Baker—some sadly for the last time.* BAKER-VAN DYKE COLLECTION

(1) A cheesecake pose for the Hawai'i Visitors Bureau. TONGG PUBLISHING *(2) Bob Hope learns the hula.* PHOEBE BEACH COLLECTION *(3) A reenactment of the landing of Kamehameha the Great at Waikīkī Beach. The first pageant, which fostered the annual Kamehameha Day celebrations, was hampered by the morality laws of the 1910s, which declared that "showing of unclad skin on the beach is immoral."* TONGG PUBLISHING *(4) Legendary singer and entertainer Don Ho gets tickled during audience participation during his famous show.* TONGG PUBLISHING *(5) The radio show Hawai'i Calls, once heard on 750 stations worldwide and broadcast live from the Moana Hotel, lured many visitors to the islands.* HAWAI'I VISITORS BUREAU PHOTO

(1) Matching-dressed tourist couples showing togetherness have always amused locals. LAURENCE HATA COLLECTION, BISHOP MUSEUM
(2) Riding the waves at Waikīkī—solo, twosomes, threesomes, board or outrigger, male or female. Circa 1945. LOUIS REYES COLLECTION (3) The renowned Hilo Hattie belts out one of her famous routines of song, dance, and humor with the Hawai'i Calls Orchestra. HAWAI'I STATE ARCHIVES (4) Don the Beachcomber welcomes novelist James Michener when the writer came to the islands in 1964 to write his epic Hawai'i. PHOEBE BEACH COLLECTION (5) President John Kennedy and Governor Burns (seated) ride in an open-air limousine in a motorcade on Kalākaua Avenue during an official visit to the islands in June of 1963. Five months later, on November 22, 1963, the President was assassinated while riding in a similar motorcade in Dallas, Texas. LAURENCE HATA COLLECTION, BISHOP MUSEUM